Poetry for Young People

Edna St. Vincent Millay

Edited by Frances Schoonmaker
Illustrated by Mike Bryce

STERLING

New York / London

To Liesl Claire Bolin,
"Into my face a miracle,"
from Renascence
FRANCES SCHOONMAKER

Thank you to my family and friends who have always believed in my work
as an artist and illustrator and have given me such tremendous support
throughout the making of this book.
For Sabrina with love.
MIKE BRYCE

Photograph on page 4 courtesy Special Collections, Vassar College Libraries, Poughkeepsie, N.Y.

Lot#:
1   3   5   7   9   10   8   6   4   2
01/10

First paperback edition published 2010 by Sterling Publishing Co., Inc.
387 Park Avenue South, New York, N.Y. 10016
Copyright © 1912, 1913, 1917, 1921, 1922, 1940, 1941, 1945, 1948, 1950
by Edna St. Vincent Millay
Copyright © 1923, 1928, 1939, 1951, 1954, 1955, 1967, 1982 by Edna St. Vincent Millay and Norma Millay
Ellis. All rights reserved. Reprinted by permission of Elizabeth Barnett, literary administrator, The Edna St.
Vincent Millay Society
Editorial matter © 1999 by Frances Schoonmaker
Illustrations © 1999 by Mike Bryce
Distributed in Canada by Sterling Publishing
℅ Canadian Manda Group, 165 Dufferin Street
Toronto, Ontario, Canada M6K 3H6

Printed in China
All rights reserved

Sterling ISBN 978-0-8069-5928-3 (trade)
Sterling ISBN 978-1-4027-7295-5 (paper)

Contents

INTRODUCTION

When Edna St. Vincent Millay was born, her family and friends called her "Vincent." It was an unusual  name, and she came by it in an unusual way. Her parents, Henry Millay and Cora Buzzelle Millay, lived in a small town in Maine. Cora Millay's brother was a sailor. One day he was in a terrible storm at sea, and he was so badly injured everyone was afraid he would die. He was taken to St. Vincent's Hospital in New York City, where he got well. Cora Millay was so happy that she named her first baby for the faraway hospital. That was on February 22, 1892. A year later, the Millays had a second daughter, Norma. Three years after that, Kathleen was born. So Vincent was the first of three girls.

Henry Millay was a high school teacher and administrator. He was good-looking and intelligent. People liked him wherever he went. Cora, Vincent's mother, was very artistic. She sang, played the piano, and loved to read. She hoped her family could enjoy these things, too. Cora wanted the girls to have piano lessons, books, and concert tickets, but there was little money for such luxuries. Henry Millay liked to gamble. He kept losing all of the extra money that might have gone for special things, and he refused to quit. So there were many quarrels between Vincent's parents. Finally, Cora asked Henry to leave if he could not do better. Vincent was seven years old. She never forgot the sight of him walking away. From that time on, the girls lived with their mother and rarely saw their father. He lived in a different town after the divorce. He was always interested in the girls and friendly with their mother, but he did not help out with money for their everyday needs. And he left their upbringing to Cora.

For three years after the divorce, Cora Millay and her daughters lived with family. They were in first one small town, then another. Cora began working as a nurse. She was not trained as nurses are today, but she could give care to sick or old people in their homes. She made enough money to rent a small house in Camden, Maine, which was Vincent's home until she grew up. Cora worked nights so she could be with the girls during the day. To earn extra money, she made hairpieces that fashionable women wore. Everyone had to work very hard to keep the family together. In those days they had to chop wood for the fires. They did not have electricity, so they had to keep oil lamps filled and their wicks trimmed. Cora had to make their clothes. And they had to heat big pots of water for laundry, which was done by hand.

It was a big job to keep a family going, but, by the time she was twelve years old, Vincent was doing it. The family needed more money. Cora could make more if she worked for people in the day as well as at night. Sometimes her patients were in another town. Then she would be away for days or weeks at a time. When Cora was at home she sewed, baked, and did laundry to make things easier for the girls.

One of the people Cora worked for was a famous musician, John Wheeler Tufts. Once Vincent went with her, and, waiting for her mother, saw Tufts's grand piano. Temptation overcame her! She began to play and sing one of her compositions. Cora was embarrassed that Vincent had been so impolite, but Tufts was delighted. He was so impressed that he insisted on giving her free lessons. Vincent was a willing student. At one time, she thought about becoming a concert pianist, but Vincent was tiny and her hands were too small. She never gave up playing the piano, though. She often said she could not get along without her music.

Some people felt sorry for the Millay family because they had so little money. But all three of the Millay girls remembered their home as a place of fun and joy. Most girls of that time were not permitted to run about the way boys were. But the Millay girls were given freedom and responsibility. They worked when they pleased and went to bed when they liked. Cora Millay believed that they could be trusted, and they could.

It was true that while Cora was gone they let the dishes pile up after dinner. Instead of washing dishes they sang songs, made up and acted out plays, or they read. When all the dishes were dirty, Vincent would organize a game or make up a song to wash dishes by—one was called "I'm the Queen of the Dishpans." They always swept and scrubbed the house before their mother came home. When it was time to clean, Vincent would yell, "Corner," and each of them would choose a corner where they began cleaning as fast as they could. They would meet in the middle and clean the fourth corner together.

Girlfriends loved to visit them to play cards, sing, and act out plays. They even helped clean the house to Vincent's games and songs. When things didn't go right, the Millay girls imagined they were better. Once, the pipes froze and burst during a cold winter night. They awoke to a kitchen floor covered with ice. They didn't sit and cry about the broken pipes and the mess they would have to clean up. Instead, they got their skates and skated around the kitchen floor!

The girls liked to pick blueberries on the hill, gather cranberries from the nearby bog, swim in the bay, and walk in the snow with their friends. Vincent loved to watch the birds, too. She kept these interests all of her life. One of her favorite spots was the top of Mount Battie, where she could look down on the bay below or to the hills beyond. Later, when she was 20 years old, she published her first poem, "Renascence." It talks about "three long mountains and a wood," and "three islands in a bay." Vincent could see all of these from the top of Mt. Battie. (The introduction to the poem may be found on page 47.)

Once, she was sitting alone on the shore by the bay. She spied a little green island just out to sea. It was within easy swimming distance. So she plunged into the water. But, as she kept swimming toward it, the island seemed farther away. Still, she kept on. She knew she could have a rest before returning to shore. When she finally reached the island she was nearly exhausted. But the "island" was not an island at all! It was a mass of seaweed that had been floating away from her. For a few moments she was terrified. There was no place to rest. Tired or not, she must swim back to shore or drown. She never forgot this experience of fighting to stay alive. She wrote many poems about death. Some people think she was remembering this experience. (One of her poems about death is on page 28.)

Edna St. Vincent Millay was writing poetry when she was five years old. The first poem she wrote down began, "One bird on a tree, One bird come to me." She kept a little poetry notebook, which she called "Poetical Works of E. Vincent Millay." She dedicated it to her mother. Cora Millay considered these works to be very important—even more important than keeping the house in order. Later, Millay wrote to her mother, "I cannot remember once in my life when you were not interested in what I was working on, or even suggested that I should put it aside for something else."

Even though they had very little money, Cora insisted on books, magazines, music, and art in the home. Mother and daughters agreed. They could get by with very little heat in the winter, but they could not get along without books. Many years later, when she had her own apartment in Greenwich Village in New York City, Vincent remembered this. She worked as an actress and writer. The Village was an exciting place, where many young artists lived, but life was not easy. Sometimes her apartment was too cold for her to write, because she could not afford to buy a ten-cent stick of wood for a fire—but she had books. She didn't eat properly either, and worked long hours into the night writing poetry, plays, and short stories. She even wrote a column in a Village paper in order to earn money. It was about living in New York. People thought it was witty and funny. She used another name, though. She didn't want people to confuse this writing with her poetry.

Edna St. Vincent Millay's poetry is about the wonder and mystery of ordinary life. She had imagination. She wrote, "I will be the gladdest thing under the sun" about an ordinary "Afternoon on a Hill" (see page 9). She watched men putting in the poles for electrical wires and saw the beauty and magic of their work. In "Men Working," she wrote, "in the back of each man's mind The respect for the pole: it is forty feet high, and weighs Two thousand pounds." (This poem may be found on page 41.) She could look at the wild swans flying over and later write, "Wild swans, come over the town, come over/ The town again, trailing your legs and crying!" (see page 46). She knew that wonder and mystery are everywhere if you just have imagination.

Who would have imagined that a young girl from a home where there was so little money could graduate from college? But someone heard her reciting her poetry and helped her to go to Vassar College. And who would have imagined that a poem that wasn't chosen for the top prize in a poetry contest would become more famous than the prize-winning poems? But Vincent's poem "Renascence," was published with the winning poems, and it was the one most noticed by poets all over the United States.

Who would have imagined that she would meet her future husband at a party that she didn't even want to go to? But many years after she had become a famous poet, Millay met Eugen Jan Boissevain at a party. And who would imagine that this wealthy businessman would give up his coffee importing business to manage things for her, so that Millay could write even more poetry? But Boissevain was a feminist (he believed men and women were equal). He said, "Anyone can buy and sell coffee, but anyone cannot write poetry."

Bad eating habits, long, late working hours, and worrying about having enough money to live on caught up with Vincent. When Bossivian first met her, he could see that she was not well and insisted that she go to the doctor. She was much worse off than even Bossivian imagined. She needed to have surgery, but she was too weak. The doctors said she might die from surgery, but without it, she was almost sure to die. So Boissevian insisted that Vincent move into his home where she could be taken care of until she was strong enough for an operation. They were married in the hospital! When she was well enough to leave the hospital, Boissevian took her around the world so she could regain her health.

For many years she had struggled to have enough money. Now she had a wealthy husband who wanted to take care of her. But Vincent was determined to pay her own bills. Her books of poetry and plays were beginning to bring in some money. She was in great demand for poetry readings. She travelled all over the United States, reading her poetry in theatres and at colleges. In 1923, she won the Pulitzer Prize, an award for great writing. It was the first time a woman had ever won the award for poetry. It gave her $1,000 and she started her own bank account. For the first time she had enough money to have a bank account. Paying her own way was part of keeping the independence Vincent wanted and needed all of her life.

The couple bought a farm in New York state, where they settled down. Boissevian took care of all the details of daily life, including looking after the house and seeing that Vincent ate properly. He answered the many letters she received, and did everything he could to keep her focused on her writing. For many years they enjoyed a quiet life together on their farm. They took long walks, looking at the wildflowers and birds. Vincent kept writing and became outspoken on politics. She had always been close to her family, and it was a terrible blow when her mother died. It was also a terrible blow when Boissevian died a few years later. He had been an ideal companion and friend for the free-spirited Vincent. On October 19, 1950, a year and a half afterward, she died quietly on the farm.

The imagination and determination that Vincent had as a little girl stayed with her all her life. Imagination and determination found their way into the many poems that we enjoy today. When she was writing, many people thought her poetry was too simple to be interesting. But others loved it, and thought it told the feelings of young people. Many say she was the most famous poet of her time. Today, there are still people who think her poems are too simple to be really great poetry. But others think that her simple words and statements show understanding and courage. They consider her one of our greatest American poets.

AFTERNOON ON A HILL

I will be the gladdest thing
    Under the sun!
I will touch a hundred flowers
    And not pick one.

I will look at cliffs and clouds
    With quiet eyes,
Watch the wind bow down the grass,
    And the grass rise.

And when lights begin to show
    Up from the town,
I will mark which must be mine,
    And then start down!

TO THE NOT IMPOSSIBLE HIM

How shall I know, unless I go
    To Cairo and Cathay,
Whether or not this blessed spot
    Is blest in every way?

Now it may be, the flower for me
    Is beneath my nose;
How shall I tell, unless I smell
    The Carthaginian rose?

The fabric of my faithful love
    No power shall dim or ravel
Whilst I stay here,—but oh, my dear,
    If I should ever travel!

Carthage—*a great city and state of the ancient*
    world, located in northern Africa; a few ruins of
    the city still remain
Cathay—*an old name for China*

THURSDAY

And if I loved you Wednesday,
    Well, what is that to you?
I do not love you Thursday—
    So much is true.

And why you come complaining
    Is more than I can see.
I loved you Wednesday,—yes—but what
    Is that to me?

TRAVEL

The railroad track is miles away,
    And the day is loud with voices speaking,
Yet there isn't a train goes by all day
    But I hear its whistle shrieking.

All night there isn't a train goes by,
    Though the night is still for sleep and dreaming,
But I see its cinders red on the sky,
    And hear its engine steaming.

My heart is warm with the friends I make,
    And better friends I'll not be knowing;
Yet there isn't a train I wouldn't take,
    No matter where it's going.

FIRST FIG

My candle burns at both ends;
   It will not last the night;
But ah, my foes, and oh, my friends—
   It gives a lovely light!

SECOND FIG

Safe upon the solid rock the ugly houses stand:
Come and see my shining palace built upon the sand!

WONDER WHERE THIS HORSESHOE WENT*

Wonder where this horseshoe went
Up and down, up and down,
Up and past the monument,
Maybe into town.

Wait a minute. "Horseshoe,
How far have you been?"
Says it's been to Salem
And halfway to Lynn.

Wonder who was in the team.
Wonder what they saw.
Wonder if they passed a bridge—
Bridge with a draw.

Says it went from one bridge
Straight upon another.
Says it took a little girl
Driving with her mother.

* from "A Very Little Sphinx"

TAVERN

I'll keep a little tavern
    Below the high hill's crest,
Wherein all grey-eyed people
    May sit them down and rest.

There shall be plates a-plenty,
    And mugs to melt the chill
Of all the grey-eyed people
    Who happen up the hill.

There sound will sleep the traveller,
    And dream his journey's end,
But I will rouse at midnight
    The falling fire to tend.

Aye, 'tis a curious fancy—
    But all the good I know
Was taught me out of two grey eyes
    A long time ago.

RECUERDO

We were very tired, we were very merry—
We had gone back and forth all night on the ferry.
It was bare and bright, and smelled like a stable—
But we looked into a fire, we leaned across a table,
We lay on a hill-top underneath the moon;
And the whistles kept blowing, and the dawn came soon.

We were very tired, we were very merry—
We had gone back and forth all night on the ferry;
And you ate an apple, and I ate a pear,
From a dozen of each we had bought somewhere;
And the sky went wan, and the wind came cold,
And the sun rose dripping, a bucketful of gold.

We were very tired, we were very merry,
We had gone back and forth all night on the ferry.
We hailed, "Good morrow, mother!" to a shawl-covered head,
And bought a morning paper, which neither of us read;
And she wept, "God bless you!" for the apples and pears,
And we gave her all our money but our subway fares.

Recuerdo—*(Spanish) Memory or souvenir*

EEL-GRASS

No matter what I say,
    All that I really love
Is the rain that flattens on the bay,
    And the eel-grass in the cove;
The jingle-shells that lie and bleach
    At the tide-line, and the trace
Of higher tides along the beach:
    Nothing in this place.

EBB

I know what my heart is like
    Since your love died:
It is like a hollow ledge
Holding a little pool
    Left there by the tide,
    A little tepid pool,
Drying inward from the edge.

tepid—*lukewarm*

17

EXILED

Searching my heart for its true sorrow,
    This is the thing I find to be:
That I am weary of words and people,
    Sick of the city, wanting the sea;

Wanting the sticky, salty sweetness
    Of the strong wind and shattered spray;
Wanting the loud sound and the soft sound
    Of the big surf that breaks all day.

Always before about my dooryard
  Marking the reach of the winter sea,
Rooted in sand and dragging drift-wood,
  Straggled the purple wild sweet-pea;

Always I climbed the wave at morning,
  Shook the sand from my shoes at night,
That now am caught beneath great buildings,
  Stricken with noise, confused with light.

If I could hear the green piles groaning
  Under the windy wooden piers,
See once again the bobbing barrels,
  And the black sticks that fence the weirs,

If I could see the weedy mussels
  Crusting the wrecked and rotting hulls,
Here once again the hungry crying
  Overhead, of the wheeling gulls,

Feel once again the shanty straining
  Under the turning of the tide,
Fear once again the rising freshet,
  Dread the bell in the fog outside,

I should be happy!—that was happy
  All day long on the coast of Maine;
I have a need to hold and handle
  Shells and anchors and ships again!

I should be happy . . . that am happy
  Never at all since I came here.
I am too long away from water.
  I have a need of water near.

weirs—*a fence or enclosure of stakes made in a river or harbor*
freshet—*a freshwater stream flowing from a river into the sea*

INLAND

People that build their houses inland,
   People that buy a plot of ground
Shaped like a house, and build a house there,
   Far from the sea-board, far from the sound

Of water sucking the hollow ledges,
   Tons of water striking the shoe,—
What do they long for, as I long for
   One salt smell of the sea once more?

People the waves have not awakened,
   Spanking the boars at the harbour's head,
What do they long for, as I long for,—
   Starting up in my inland bed,

Beating the narrow walls, and finding
   Neither a window nor a door,
Screaming to God for death by drowning,—
   One salt taste of the sea once more?

KIN TO SORROW

Am I kin to Sorrow,
    That so oft
Falls the knocker of my door—
    Neither loud nor soft,
But as long accustomed—
    Under Sorrow's hand?
Marigolds around the step
    And rosemary stand,
And then comes Sorrow—
    And what does Sorrow care
For the rosemary
    Or the marigolds there?
Am I kin to Sorrow?
    Are we kin?
That so oft upon my door—
    Oh, come in!

CITY TREES

The trees along this city street,
　　Save for the traffic and the trains,
Would make a sound as thin and sweet
　　As trees in country lanes.

And people standing in their shade
　　Out of a shower, undoubtedly
Would hear such music as is made
　　Upon a country tree.

Oh, little leaves that are so dumb
　　Against the shrieking city air,
I watch you when the wind has come,—
　　I know what sound is there.

THE SNOW STORM

No hawk hangs over in this air:
The urgent snow is everywhere.
The wing adroiter than a sail
Must lean away from such a gale,
Abandoning its straight intent,
Or else expose tough ligament
And tender flesh to what before
Meant dampened feathers, nothing more.

Forceless upon our backs there fall
Infrequent flakes hexagonal,
Devised in many a curious style
To charm our safety for a while,
Where close to earth like micc we go
Under the horizontal snow.

adroiter—*more skillful, neat, or clever than someone else*
ligament—*fastener or bond; in the human body, a ligament is a tough band of tissue that holds joints or organs in place*

RAIN COMES DOWN

Rain comes down
And hushes the town.
And where is the voice that I heard crying?

Snow settles
Over the nettles.
Where is the voice that I heard crying?

Sand at last
On the drifting mast.
And where is the voice that I heard crying?

Earth now
On the busy brow.
And where is the voice that I heard crying?

DEPARTURE

It's little I care what path I take,
And where it leads it's little I care;
But out of this house, lest my heart break,
I must go, and off somewhere.

It's little I know what's in my heart,
What's in my mind it's little I know,
But there's that in me must up and start,
And it's little I care where my feet go.

I wish I could walk for a day and a night,
And find me at dawn in a desolate place
With never the rut of a road in sight,
Nor the roof of a house, nor the eyes of a face.

I wish I could walk till my blood should spout,
And drop me, never to stir again,
On a shore that is wide, for the tide is out,
And the weedy rocks are bare to the rain.

But dump or dock, where the path I take
Brings up, it's little enough I care;
And it's little I'd mind the fuss they'll make,
Huddled dead in a ditch somewhere.

"Is something the matter, dear," she said,
"That you sit at your work so silently?"
"No, mother, no, 'twas a knot in my thread.
There goes the kettle, I'll make the tea."

THE BUCK IN THE SNOW

White sky, over the hemlocks bowed with snow,
Saw you not at the beginning of evening the antlered buck and
      his doe
Standing in the apple-orchard? I saw them. I saw them
      suddenly go,
Tails up, with long leaps lovely and slow,
Over the stone-wall into the wood of hemlocks bowed with
      snow.

Now lies he here, his wild blood scalding the snow.

How strange a thing is death, bringing to his knees, bringing
      to his antlers
The buck in the snow.
How strange a thing,—a mile away by now, it may be,
Under the heavy hemlocks that as the moments pass
Shift their loads a little, letting fall a feather of snow—
Life, looking out attentive from the eyes of the doe.

SONNET

If I should learn, in some quite casual way,
That you were gone, not to return again—
Read from the back-page of a paper, say,
Held by a neighbor in a subway train,
How at the corner of this avenue
And such a street (so are the papers filled)
A hurrying man, who happened to be you,
At noon today had happened to be killed—
I should not cry aloud—I could not cry
Aloud, or wring my hands in such a place—
I should but watch the station lights rush by
With a more careful interest on my face;
Or raise my eyes and read with greater care
Where to store furs and how to treat the hair.

CHORUS

Give away her gowns,
Give away her shoes;
She has no more use
For her fragrant gowns;
Take them all down,
Blue, green, blue,
Lilac, pink, blue,
From their padded hangers;
She will dance no more
In her narrow shoes;
Sweep her narrow shoes
From the closet floor.

DIRGE WITHOUT MUSIC

I am not resigned to the shutting away of loving hearts
      in the hard ground.
So it is, and so it will be, for so it has been, time out
      of mind:
Into the darkness they go, the wise and the lovely.
      Crowned with lilies and with laurel they go; but
      I am not resigned.

Lovers and thinkers, into the earth with you.
Be one with the dull, the indiscriminate dust.
A fragment of what you felt, of what you knew,
A formula, a phrase remains,—but the best is lost.

The answers quick and keen, the honest look, the
      laughter, the love,—
They are gone. They are gone to feed the roses.
      Elegant and curled
In the blossom. Fragrant is the blossom. I know. But I
      do not approve.
More precious was the light in your eyes than all the
      roses in the world.

Down, down, down into the darkness of the grave
Gently they go, the beautiful, the tender, the kind;
Quietly they go, the intelligent, the witty, the brave.
I know. But I do not approve. And I am not resigned.

BLIGHT

Hard seeds of hate I planted
  That should by now be grown,—
Rough stalks, and from thick stamens
  A poisonous pollen blown,
And odours rank, unbreathable
  From dark corollas thrown!

At dawn from my damp garden
  I shook the chilly dew;
The thin boughs locked behind me
  That sprang to let me through;
The blossoms slept,—I sought a place
  Where nothing lovely grew.

And there, when day was breaking,
  I knelt and looked around:
The light was near, the silence
  Was palpitant with sound;
I drew my hate from out my breast
  And thrust it in the ground.

Oh, ye so fiercely tended,
  Ye little seeds of hate!
I bent above your growing
  Early and noon and late,
Yet are ye drooped and pitiful,—
  I cannot rear ye straight!

The sun seeks out my garden,
  No nook is left in shade,
No mist nor mold nor mildew
  Endures on any blade,
Sweet rain slants under every bough:
  Ye falter, and ye fade.

stamens—*part of a plant that helps*
  produce seeds.
corollas—*the little leaves or petals that*
  form the inner envelope of a flower
palpitant—*throbbing*

THE BEAN-STALK

Ho, Giant! This is I!
I have built me a bean-stalk into your sky!
La,—but it's lovely, up so high!

This is how I came,—I put
Here my knee, there my foot,
Up and up, from shoot to shoot—
And the blessèd bean-stalk thinning
Like the mischief all the time,
Till it took me rocking, spinning,
In a dizzy, sunny circle,
Making angles with the root,
Far and out above the cackle
Of the city I was born in,
Till the little dirty city
In the light so sheer and sunny
Shone as dazzling bright and pretty
As the money that you find
In a dream of finding money—
What a wind! What a morning!—

Till the tiny, shiny city,
When I shot a glance below,
Shaken with a giddy laughter,
Sick and blissfully afraid,
Was a dew-drop on a blade,
And a pair of moments after
Was the whirling guess I made,—
And the wind was like a whip
Cracking past my icy ears,
And my hair stood out behind,
And my eyes were full of tears,
Wide-open and cold,
More tears than they could hold,
The wind was blowing so,
And my teeth were in a row,
Dry and grinning,

And I felt my foot slip,
And I scratched the wind and whined,
And I clutched the stalk and jabbered,
With my eyes shut blind,—
What a wind! What a wind!

Your broad sky, Giant,
Is the shelf of a cupboard;
I make bean-stalks, I'm
A builder, like yourself,
But bean-stalks is my trade,
I couldn't make a shelf,
Don't know how they're made,
Now, a bean-stalk is more pliant—
La, what a climb!

pliant—*flexible*

WRAITH

"Thin Rain, whom are you haunting,
That you haunt my door?"
Surely it is not I she's wanting . . .
Someone living here before!
"Nobody's in the house but me:
You may come in if you like and see."

Thin as thread, with exquisite fingers,—
Ever seen her, any of you?—
Grey shawl, and leaning on the wind,
And the garden showing through?

Glimmering eyes,—and silent, mostly,
Sort of a whisper, sort of a purr,
Asking something, asking it over,
If you get a sound from her.—

Ever see her, any of you?—
Strangest thing I've ever known,—
Every night since I moved in,
And I came to be alone.

"Thin Rain, hush with your knocking!
You may not come in!
This is I that you hear rocking;
Nobody's with me, nor has been!"

Curious, how she tried the window,—
Odd, the way she tries the door,
Wonder just what sort of people
Could have had this house before . . .

wraith—*a ghost*

36

THE LITTLE GHOST

I knew her for a little ghost
　　That in my garden walked;
The wall is high—higher than most—
　　And the green gate was locked.

And yet I did not think of that
　　Till after she was gone—
I knew her by the broad white hat,
　　All ruffled, she had on.

By the dear ruffles round her feet,
　　By her small hands that hung
In their lace mitts, austere and sweet,
　　Her gown's white folds among.

I watched to see if she would stay,
　　What she would do—and oh!
She looked as if she liked the way
　　I let my garden grow!

She bent above my favourite mint
　　With conscious garden grace,
She smiled and smiled—there was no hint
　　Of sadness in her face.

She held her gown on either side
　　To let her slippers show,
And up the walk she went with pride,
　　The way great ladies go.

And where the wall is built in new,
　　And is of ivy bare,
She paused—then opened and passed through
　　A gate that once was there.

austere—*harsh, grave, or forbidding*

THE DEATH OF AUTUMN

When reeds are dead and a straw to thatch the marshes,
And feathered pampas-grass rides into the wind
Like agèd warriors westward, tragic, thinned
Of half their tribe; and over the flattened rushes,
Stripped of its secret, open, stark and bleak,
Blackens afar the half-forgotten creek,—
Then leans on me the weight of the year, and crushes
My heart. I know that Beauty must ail and die,
And will be born again,—but ah, to see
Beauty stiffened, staring up at the sky!
Oh, Autumn! Autumn!—What is the Spring to me?

ASSAULT

I had forgotten how the frogs must sound
After a year of silence, else I think
I should not so have ventured forth alone
At dusk upon this unfrequented road.

I am waylaid by Beauty. Who will walk
Between me and the crying of the frogs?
Oh, savage Beauty, suffer me to pass,
That am a timid woman, on her way
From one house to another!

MEN WORKING

Charming, the movement of girls about a May-pole in May,
Weaving the coloured ribbons in and out,
Charming; youth is charming, youth is fair.

But beautiful the movement of men striking pikes
Into the end of a black pole, and slowly
Raising it out of the damp grass and up into the air,
The clean strike of the pike into the pole: beautiful.

Joe is the boss, but Ed or Bill will say,
"No, Joe; we can't get it that way—
We've got to take it from here. Are you okay
On your side, Joe?" "Yes," says the boss. "Okay."

The clean strike of the pike into the pole—*"That's it!"*
"Ground your pikes!"

The grounded pikes about the rising black pole, beautiful.
"Ed, you'd better get under here with me!" "I'm
Under!"

"That's it!"
"Ground your pikes!"

Joe says, "Now, boys, don't heave
Too hard—we've got her—but you, Ed, you and Mike,
You'll have to hold her from underneath while Bill
Shifts his pike—she wants to fall downhill;
We've got her all right, but we've got her on a slight
Slant."
"That's it!"—"Mike,
About six feet lower this time."
"That's it!"

"Ground your pikes!"

One by one the pikes are moved about the pole, more beautiful
Than coloured ribbons weaving.

The clean strike of the pike into the pole; each man
Depending on the skill
And the balance, both of body and of mind,

Of each of the others; in the back of each man's mind
The respect for the pole; it is forty feet high, and weighs
Two thousand pounds.

In the front of each man's mind: "She's going to go
Exactly where we want her to go: this pole
Is going to go into that seven-foot hole we dug
For her
To stand in."

This was in the deepening dusk of a July night.
They were putting in the poles: bringing the electric light.

GOD'S WORLD

O World, I cannot hold thee close enough!
   Thy winds, thy wide grey skies!
   Thy mists, that roll and rise!
Thy woods, this autumn day, that ache and sag
And all but cry with colour! That gaunt crag
To crush! To lift the lean of the black bluff!
World, World, I cannot get thee close enough!

Long have I known a glory in it all,
   But never knew I this:
   Here such a passion is
As stretcheth me apart,—Lord, I do fear
Thou'st made the world too beautiful this year;
My soul is all but out of me,—let fall
No burning leaf; prithee, let no bird call.

JOURNEY

Ah, could I lay me down in this long grass
And close my eyes, and let the quiet wind
Blow over me—I am so tried, so tired
Of passing pleasant places! All my life,
Following Care along the dusty road,
Have I looked back at loveliness and sighed;
Yet at my hand an unrelenting hand
Tugged ever, and I passed. All my life long
Over my shoulder have I looked at peace;
And now I fain would lie in this long grass
And close my eyes.
                            Yet onward!
                                          Cat-birds call
Through the long afternoon, and creeks at dusk
Are guttural. Whip-poor-wills wake and cry,
Drawing the twilight close about their throats.
Only my heart makes answer. Eager vines
Go up the rocks and wait; flushed apple-trees

Pause in their dance and break the ring for me;
Dim, shady wood-roads, redolent of fern
And bayberry, that through sweet bevies thread
Of round-faced roses, pink and petulant,
Look back and beckon ere they disappear.
Only my heart, only my heart responds.

Yet, ah, my path is sweet on either side
All through the dragging day,—sharp underfoot
And hot, and like dead mist the dry dust hangs—
But far, oh, far as passionate eye can reach,
And long, ah, long as rapturous eye can cling,
The world is mine: blue hill, still silver lake,
Broad field, bright flower, and the long white
          road;
A gateless garden, and an open path;
My feet to follow, and my heart to hold.

guttural—*a sound coming from the throat*   redolent—*sweet-smelling, fragrant*   bevies—*a company or collection of things*
petulant—*to show peevish impatience*   rapturous—*wildly joyful*

WHEN THE YEAR GROWS OLD

I cannot but remember
   When the year grows old—
October—November—
   How she disliked the cold!

She used to watch the swallows
   Go down across the sky,
And turn from the window
   With a little sharp sigh.

And often when the brown leaves
   Were brittle on the ground,
And the wind in the chimney
   Made a melancholy sound,

She had a look about her
   That I wish I could forget—
The look of a scared thing
   Sitting in a net!

Oh, beautiful at nightfall
   The soft spitting snow!
And beautiful the bare boughs
   Rubbing to and fro!

But the roaring of the fire,
   And the warmth of fur,
And the boiling of the kettle
   Were beautiful to her!

I cannot but remember
   When the year grows old—
October—November—
   How she disliked the cold!

WILD SWANS

I looked in my heart while the wild swans went over.
And what did I see I had not seen before?
Only a question less or a question more;
Nothing to match the flight of wild birds flying.
Tiresome heart, forever living and dying,
House without air, I leave you and lock your door.
Wild swans, come over the town, come over
The town again, trailing your legs and crying!

RENASCENCE*

All I could see from where I stood
Was three long mountains and a wood;
I turned and looked another way,
And saw three islands in a bay.
So with my eyes I traced the line
Of the horizon, thin and fine,
Straight around till I was come
Back to where I'd started from;
And all I saw from where I stood
Was three long mountains and a wood.

The introduction to a longer poem
renascence—*rebirth or renewal*

Index